Pebble™ Plus

Máquinas maravillosas/Mighty Machines

Camiones de bomberos/Fire Trucks

por/by Carol K. Lindeen

Traducción/Translation: Martín Luis Guzmán Ferrer, Ph.D.
Editor Consultor/Consulting Editor: Dra. Gail Saunders-Smith

Capstone
press

Mankato, Minnesota

Pebble Plus is published by Capstone Press,
151 Good Counsel Drive, P.O. Box 669, Mankato, Minnesota 56002.
www.capstonepress.com

1 2 3 4 5 6 11 10 09 08 07 06

Library of Congress Cataloging-in-Publication Data
Lindeen, Carol K., 1976–
 [Fire trucks. Spanish & English]
 Camiones de bomberos/de Carol K. Lindeen=Fire trucks/by Carol K. Lindeen.
 p. cm.—(Pebble plus. Máquinas maravillosas=Pebble plus. Mighty machines)
 Includes index.
 ISBN-13: 978-0-7368-5873-1 (hardcover)
 ISBN-10: 0-7368-5873-3 (hardcover)
 I. Title. II. Series: Pebble plus. Máquinas maravillosas.
TH9372.L5618 2005
628.9—dc22   2005019055

Editorial Credits
Martha E. H. Rustad, editor; Jenny Marks, bilingual editor; Eida del Risco, Spanish copy editor; Molly Nei, set
   designer; Kate Opseth and Ted Williams, book designers; Jo Miller, photo researcher; Scott Thoms, photo
   editor

Photo Credits
Capstone Press/Gary Sundermeyer, cover; Karon Dubke, 14–15
Corbis/George Hall, 7
Folio Inc./David Frazier, 20–21
George Hall Photography LLC/Code Red/Dave Dubowski, 5, 18–19; George Hall, 12–13; John Cetrino, 8–9
Index Stock Imagery/Tom Ross, 11
OneBlueShoe, 1
911 Pictures, 17

**Pebble Plus thanks the Mankato Fire Department in Mankato, Minnesota, and members of the
Mapleton Fire Department in Mapleton, Minnesota, for their assistance with this book.**

Note to Parents and Teachers

The Mighty Machines set supports national standards related to science, technology,
and society. This book describes and illustrates fire trucks. The images support early
readers in understanding the text. The repetition of words and phrases helps early
readers learn new words. This book also introduces early readers to subject-specific
vocabulary words, which are defined in the Glossary section. Early readers may need
assistance to read some words and to use the Table of Contents, Glossary, Internet Sites,
and Index sections of the book.

Table of Contents

Tabla de contenidos

What Are Fire Trucks?

Fire trucks are vehicles

that firefighters use

to put out fires.

¿Qué son los camiones de bomberos?

Los camiones de bomberos son

vehículos que usan los bomberos

para apagar incendios.

Fire Truck Parts

Fire trucks have

flashing lights and sirens.

They warn cars

to get out of the way.

Las partes de los camiones de bomberos

Los camiones de bomberos tienen

luces centellantes y sirenas.

Les advierten a los autos que

dejen el camino libre.

Fire trucks have hoses.
Firefighters hook hoses
to hydrants to get water.

Los camiones de bomberos
tienen mangueras. Los bomberos
enroscan las mangueras a
los hidrantes para tener agua.

Fire trucks have ladders.
Firefighters climb ladders
to get to fires.

Los camiones de bomberos
tienen escaleras. Los bomberos
se suben a las escaleras para
acercarse al fuego.

To the Rescue

The alarm rings at the
fire station. Firefighters get
in the fire trucks.
They rush to the fire.

Al rescate

La alarma suena en la estación
de bomberos. Los bomberos
se suben a los camiones.
Enseguida corren al incendio.

One firefighter drives
the fire truck.
She sits in the cab.
Other firefighters
ride in the back.

Uno de los bomberos conduce
el camión de bomberos. Se sienta
en la cabina. Los demás bomberos
van detrás.

Fire fighters jump

out of the truck.

They pull hoses

out of the truck.

Los bomberos salen rápidamente

del camión de bomberos.

Jalan las mangueras fuera

del camión.

Water flows through
the hose from the hydrant.
Firefighters use tools on their
fire truck to stop the fire.

El agua corre por dentro de
la manguera enroscada al hidrante.
Los bomberos usan sus herramientas
para apagar el fuego.

Firefighters use fire trucks
to help people in emergencies.

Los bomberos usan los camiones
para ayudar a las personas en
las emergencias.

Glossary

alarm—a buzzer or bell that gives a warning or signal

cab—the driver's area of a large truck or machine

emergency—something that happens with no warning and requires action right away

fire station—a building where fire trucks are kept; firefighters work and sometimes live at a fire station.

hydrant—a large outdoor pipe connected to a water supply; firefighters use hydrants to help fight fires.

siren—an object that makes a very loud sound as a warning

vehicle—something that carries people or goods from one place to another; fire trucks, ambulances, and police cars are types of vehicles.

Glosario

alarma—timbre o campana que señala que hay peligro

cabina—lugar donde se sienta el conductor de una camión grande o una máquina

emergencia—situación inesperada y peligrosa que requiere actuar enseguida

estación de bomberos—edificio donde están los camiones de bomberos; los bomberos trabajan y viven algunas veces en la estación de bomberos.

hidrante—tubo en la calle conectado al servicio de agua; los bomberos usan los hidrantes para apagar los incendios.

sirena—objeto que hace un ruido muy fuerte como señal de peligro

vehículo—cualquier cosa que lleva personas o bienes de un lugar a otro; los camiones de bomberos, ambulancias y patrullas de policía son diferentes tipos de vehículos.

Internet Sites

FactHound offers a safe, fun way to find Internet sites related to this book. All of the sites on FactHound have been researched by our staff.

Here's how:

1) Visit *www.facthound.com*

2) Type in this special code **0736836535** for age-appropriate sites. Or enter a search word related to this book for a more general search.

3) Click on the **FETCH IT** button.

FactHound will fetch the best sites for you!

Sitios de Internet

FactHound te ofrece una manera segura y divertida para encontrar sitios de Internet relacionados con este libro. Todos los sitios de FactHound han sido investigados por nuestro equipo. Es posible que los sitios no estén en español.

Así:

1) Ve a *www.facthound.com*

2) Teclea la clave especial **0736836535** para los sitios apropiados por edad. O teclea una palabra relacionada con este libro para una búsqueda más general.

3) Clic en el botón de **FETCH IT**.

¡FactHound buscará los mejores sitios para ti!

Index

Índice